D0808964

THÉ HOLY SPIRIT IS NOT A BIRD

TY BUCKINGHAM

THE HOLY SPIRIT IS NOT A BIRD

Copyright © 2016 Ty Buckingham

Published by:
Oliver Royal Publishing

Printed in the United States of America.

All rights reserved. Under international copyright law, no part of this publication may be reproduced, stored, or transmitted by any means—electronic, mechanical, photographic (photocopy), recording or otherwise—without written permission from the Publisher.

Edited by Candice Tyer, LLC.

Cover design by Michael Buckingham

International Standard Book Number:
978-0-692-80842-9

Library of Congress Catalog Card Number Pending.

To my incredibly attractive wife, Rebecca, who has not only transcended the definition of beauty and elegance, but has eternally changed my perspective on what love is.

The best is yet to come.

THE HOLY SPIRIT IS NOT A BIRD

CONTENTS

THE HOLY SPIRIT IS NOT A BIRD

FOREWORD

BY TIM ENLOE

Ty and Rebecca Buckingham are passionate and powerful young leaders who you need to interact with!

I first met Ty when he was a college student and was immediately impressed with his hunger for God and interest in the work of the Holy Spirit. He had received healing in one of our conferences and emailed me afterwards to try to connect; he was looking for someone to answer his questions about the Spirit and healing. Though our ministry had a mentoring program, we were not looking for any more students to participate at that time, but Ty was persistent!

We eventually began to converse regularly and I quickly discovered that he was a man of prayer, the Word and passion for the Holy Spirit. I found Ty's questions to be deeply reflective and practical, with the end result always being about fulfilling God's call on his life.

After about two years, he took several ministry trips with us where I was able to see how fluently he flowed in the things of the Spirit. Knowledge, healing and words of prophecy just seemed to flow naturally out of Ty's life with astounding results. I remember one specific night at an Assemblies of God district family camp when person after person was instantly healed when Ty prayed for them; it was an electric moment.

We first met Rebecca just after she and Ty were engaged; to say that we were impressed would be an understatement! Rebecca is an incredibly gifted minister on her own (as a worship pastor at one of America's largest multi-cultural charismatic churches). However, her contagious passion for the Holy Spirit and the miraculous profoundly affects those around her. She and Ty partner together in ministry as speakers and minister in the anointing for healing together—with extraordinary results.

Having known Ty as someone I mentored, a friend and a ministry associate, and believing in his ministry one hundred percent, I would like to commend this book to you. You will be changed by the truths he unpacks, and challenged by the true stories of the miraculous he tells. Your faith will be stretched and your hunger will grow; you will not want to settle for anything less than God's best in your life!

Tim Enloe
Conference Speaker/Author
Enloe Ministries
www.enloeministries.org

INTRODUCTION

I have seen the Holy Spirit do some amazing things, but an interaction I had with a woman at Walmart impacted me more than most. This lady wasn't just healed of an issue; she had a miraculous encounter with God. It all started when I realized that a movie that I wanted to see was available to purchase and I drove to Walmart for what I thought would be a quick trip.

I walked to the back of the store where the electronic department was, and I met an employee who helped me find what I was looking for. She began to check me out, and I was ready to get home and watch the movie as soon as possible. The Holy Spirit had other plans. As the woman scanned the movie, I felt Him tell me to pray for her left knee. In all honesty I just wanted to get home, watch the movie and eat some popcorn, but I could tell something extraordinary was about to occur.

I paid and proceeded to tell the young lady that I had this feeling that I should pray for her left knee. She looked at me as if she had seen some sort of ghost. I reassured her that it was normal, and that God was simply showing her that He is real and wants to love on her. She reluctantly agreed and I asked her what her pain was on a scale of zero to ten — zero being no pain and ten being the worst pain of her life. She told me that not only was it at a seven, but the pain was in both knees. I started to pray for her in the middle of Walmart and God began to move on this woman's life. I didn't have to yell, push or do anything outside of calmly pray that God would do what He loves to do — heal the hurting.

I finished praying after about a minute and asked her what her pain was, reassuring her that even if the pain was still the same that it was okay. She laughed a little and told me that the pain went down from a seven to a four! I excitedly told her that God was clearly showing her His love, and she agreed in amazement. I asked if I could pray again because,

There has never been the slightest doubt in my mind that the God who started this great work in you would keep at it and bring it to a flourishing finish.
Philippians 1:6 MSG

She allowed me to pray for her again, and afterward she burst out in astonishment that the pain was at a two! The pain that just minutes before was at a seven was at a two because of the love and power of the Holy Spirit.

Right as I was about to pray one last time to see her pain go down to a zero, the Holy Spirit told me something else to say and I listened. I told the young lady that I felt as though the problems with her knees were actually connected to a bigger issue. I asked if I could also pray for that too. Her whole persona changed as she began to affirm what the Holy Spirit had told me. She began telling me that her knees weren't the only thing that had been hurting. I came to find out that this young lady had an incurable disease called lupus, her pain was in her feet and her knees, and she was diagnosed seven years earlier.

The Holy Spirit was clearly up to something, so I began to pray for her in the same manner that I was praying before. I believed for a miracle. After praying a very simple prayer for no longer than thirty seconds, the woman started jumping up and down. I had no idea what was going on so I asked her what she was feeling. Like a child beaming with joy on Christmas morning, she told me that for the first time in over seven years she could stand without any pain and the lupus was gone!

What I love about the Holy Spirit is

that He is always looking to love on people in amazing ways. Sometimes He does it through healing, an encouraging word or some other function of His love, but one thing is biblically certain: the Holy Spirit is relentlessly pursuing an authentic relationship with us.

This book is an honest compilation of experiences and biblical principles about the Holy Spirit, and the adventure we can have with Him. This story of hearing things from the Holy Spirit that only God would know, or praying for a sick person who is instantly healed are things that anyone with the Holy Spirit can do. This book is about that kind of relationship that we can have with Him, and what it looks like to be a part of these kinds of miracles.

At the end of each chapter is a quick opportunity to reflect on what you read so that you may push forward in your relationship with the Holy Spirit. The back of this book has some pages where you can begin to write down the things that the Holy Spirit does to and through you.

I believe this book can be filled with your stories too — stories about seeing things you prayed for, and growing in your relationship with the One who makes those miracles happen. I pray that this book doesn't just grow your faith through reading my stories, but that it would ignite your faith so that you have your own.

ONE: THE HOLY SPIRIT IS NOT A BIRD

Do you remember "bring your pet to school day"? It was often in the early years of elementary school, or even preschool, when kids would bring in their most beloved pet and show it off to their friends. There seemed to always be a couple of stereotypes on those days. First was the blue eyed, blonde haired boy from the better part of town who would bring in his Labrador Retriever, which was imported from Europe and bought by his parents. The dog, of course still a puppy and no where close to being potty trained, would run all over the classroom bumping into shelves making all their contents fall to the floor. Every one of the kids would chase the dog to try to get just one touch of that platinum fur.

The second stereotype was the girl who would not just bring in her cat, but would talk to it as if it were a person. This was the girl every guy ended up having a crush on in high school, but in elementary school her best friend was Cupcake the Cat. The cat was lazy and quite fat, and was really a bore to most of the students. Then there was the kid who brought a bird.

I think if we are honest with ourselves we can understand the idea of having a pet. As I write this book, my wife and I have a cat named Oliver. All he does is sleep and occasionally sit up like a human, so I can understand the pet life. As a simple rule of thumb, I would say that dogs and cats are the most acceptable pets, but a bird as a pet is something I will never understand. Here's my problem with a pet bird: they fly around — usually in a panic — trying to escape the small room or cage you have them in; they make the loudest sounds at the most inconvenient times; and they make a mess of everything if they ever get let out of their cage. Often times the first thing people do when they hear about the Holy Spirit is they picture a dove or a bird of sorts, and this just is not an accurate portrayal of the Holy Spirit.

I find it quite humorous at times when people will ask me questions like, "So what is the Holy Spirit"? I understand what they are trying to ask, but I really believe that most Christians think this way — that the Holy Spirit is a what rather than a who. The Holy Spirit is most certainly not a what...or a bird.

WHO IS THE HOLY SPIRIT?

While reading the Bible there are times where we can easily misunderstand what is literal and what is figurative; however, this isn't one of those scenarios. The most notable passage where people get this idea that the Holy Spirit is a bird or something like that is in the book of Matthew.

> When He had been baptized, Jesus came up immediately from the water; and behold, the heavens were opened to Him, and He saw the Spirit of God descending like a dove.
> Matthew 3:16 NKJ

There is an important word you need to give attention to in this passage; it is the word *like*. That word is a comparative to the word dove, saying that the Holy Spirit is not an actual dove. However, it is saying that the Holy Spirit was descending like what we would best describe as a dove. If you have ever seen a miracle or experienced the heaviness of God's presence, you know that it is truly indescribable, even if what you are feeling can be seen.

Even when seeing something very simple to describe, like someone getting out of a wheelchair, it is often hard to put what is really happening into words. Not if, but when you have an encounter with the Holy Spirit you can try to describe it, but you may find that you will have to compare it to the closest thing you can relate it to in an earthly sense. That's where the bird comes in.

You can see the same thing in the upper room passage when the Holy Spirit came on Pentecost. This may be hard to believe, but fire wasn't actually on people's heads. The passage in Acts 2 regarding this fire says, "as of fire", which clearly tells us that it isn't actual fire but something that resembled or was best described as such. Now what this really was I do not know, but it was something of the great example of the Spirit's power and reality.

When I first came to understand who the Holy Spirit is, the first thing that I had to do was to personify Him — to come to the understanding that He's not a bird, an angel or some ghost. He is God, and He is as much God as Jesus is. When we can understand Him as a Him, instead of Him as a what, we start letting down our guard regarding what He wants to do in our lives. Then the relationship can become real and honest. If we can agree that the Holy Spirit is not a bird, or an it, then who is He? And when did He come into the picture?

What many people don't notice when reading the Bible is how often the Holy Spirit is actually mentioned, whether directly or through symbolic representation. The first time we see the Holy Spirit in the Bible is actually in the second verse written:

> Now the earth was formless and empty, darkness was over the surface of the deep, and the Spirit of God was hovering over the waters.
> Genesis 1:2 NIV

That's the first time we see the Holy Spirit (or the Spirit of God — it's the same thing, just different vernacular) doing something, and that is important because in a way the Holy Spirit is the verb of the Trinity. Jesus, of course, did great things but we must understand that He did them through the power of the Holy Spirit. If you read through the gospels you will notice that there isn't one recorded miracle until after Jesus receives the Holy Spirit. This in no way makes what Jesus did small, but actually makes Him much bigger. We should be encouraged because the same Spirit that was in Jesus performing miracles in the Bible is that same Spirit that we have in us. It is that Spirit, that person of the trinity of God, that we can commune and have relationship with on a daily basis.

HOLY GHOST?

The Holy Spirit is not a ghost. I don't see this as often anymore, but once there was normality in calling the Holy Spirit the Holy Ghost. One reason for this was because the

King James Version of the Bible titled Him as such; however, it is not an accurate depiction of who He is. When you think of a ghost the first thing you probably think of is a little boy on Halloween with a sheet over his head that has two holes cut out for his eyes. Some people think of scary, paranormal movies in which crazy things happen to people and they are controlled without their consent.

There is no need to fear; one thing that the Holy Spirit doesn't do is scare people like that.

For God has not given us the spirit of fear, but of power and of love and of a sound mind.
2 Timothy 1:7 NKJ

The Holy Spirit will never do anything to scare us. That's not to say He won't take us out of our comfort zones, but the Bible also says that the Holy Spirit is a comforter to us (John 14:26).

I was preaching a healing service at a youth group in Atlanta and had a very vivid leading from God. Near the end of my message the Holy Spirit spoke to me to mention something that was out of my comfort zone. The Holy Spirit very promptly told me to ask if there was a kid who'd had a soccer injury the previous week, and if it had been causing constant knee pain. It is not unusual for God to do this in one of our services, but for some reason I started fearing what would happen if the kid weren't in the service and what would happen if I called for him and no one responded. In essence, I was afraid of being embarrassed so I didn't say anything.

I finished the prayer and kids began to pack the altars. We saw almost one hundred kids instantly healed that weekend, but there was one that stood out — yup, you guessed it — the soccer player.

As I was concluding praying for students, the last to be prayed for was a seventh grader who was obviously filled with faith. I began to ask him what was going on. He told me that the week prior he'd gotten a soccer injury and his knee had been hurting him constantly. I actually saw him as he slightly limped to the altar. So of course two things happened in my mind. First, I felt absolutely ridiculous for not saying anything during my message because God was right (surprise). Secondly, it made realize that I should never question the Holy Spirit when He says to do something, because as long as I know what I'm hearing is of God and is biblically solid then I should go for it.

After I went through this quick but humbling experience, I apologized to the boy for not speaking up. He didn't seem to care all that much and humorously asked me if we could still pray even though I had previously kept quiet. I laughed with him and then began to pray. The student was immediately healed of all pain, was able to run to his friends, and went to go play basketball immediately after the prayer time.

The Holy Spirit isn't a ghost. He never wants to scare us; He wants to push us to a new level of relationship with Him. Often times He will do things like what happened in the story above, which would've actually given the young man even more confidence to respond and experience God in a more powerful way. Next time you feel like the Holy Spirit is telling you to do something — and it aligns with God's Word — do it!

The Holy Spirit is not a bird; He's not about making messes with our lives. In fact, He's about cleaning up our lives and making them better. The Holy Spirit isn't a ghost. He is not one to cause fear of things, but rather to give us a great awe of God and His love. The Holy Spirit is God; He was, and is, and is to come just as God the Father is. We get the privilege and adventure of getting to know Him!

CH 1 REFLECTION

WRITE ABOUT THE HOLY SPIRIT

Write a sentence or two about what part of the Holy Spirit you want to know better. Remeber that this book is a jump-start to a relationship with Him, so write down what you want to know about Him. Then pray about what you write as you read this book and, if you listen to Him, I would be willing to bet that by the end you will know Him better in that area.

_____

_____

_____

_____

_____

_____

_____

_____

_____

TWO: PERSONALITY OF THE HOLY SPIRIT

The Holy Spirit is a part of the Trinity. While the word Trinity isn't in the Bible, it is by far the best way to describe the relationship between God the Father, Son and Holy Spirit. In order to fully understand the personality of the Holy Spirit, there must be an understanding of the relationship He has in correlation to the Son and the Father. This may sound silly, but for me the simplest way to think of it is like a PB&J sandwich. There is bread, peanut butter and jelly; together they are PB&J. Is there jelly? Yes. Is there peanut butter? Yes. Is there bread? Yes. They are all separate but they become one if you want a real PB&J. Understanding the deeper things about God can feel difficult or confusing; we are not supposed to understand everything about God. We should understand who God is and that the Holy Spirit is God; therefore, let's get to know Him.

When I use the word personality in regard to the Holy Spirit, what I mean is He has attributes of His personhood — all this to understand that He is more real than you may believe. In order to understand a personality we must define what makes a person (rather than an animal or some other arbitrary identifier). What make a personality are three basic elements: cognition, decision and emotion. His ways are higher than our ways, and His personally and personality factors are also superior to ours.

HOW THE HOLY SPIRIT THINKS

First is how the Holy Spirit thinks intellectually, and there are two verses that clearly show this:

Now God has revealed these things to us by the Spirit, for the Spirit searches everything, even the depths of God. For who among men knows the thoughts of a man except the spirit of the man that is in him? In the same way, no one knows the thoughts of God except the Spirit of God.
1 Corinthians 2:10-11 HCSB

As you can see from these passages, the Holy Spirit values knowing both God and us. He's not some professor just wanting to know for the sake of knowing; He wants to know for the sake of loving. In any relationship the only way there is growth is through knowledge of and experience with someone. When I married my wonderful wife, Rebecca, I knew everything I needed to know in order to marry her: her core values, her relationship with God and FICO score (just kidding, but you see what I'm saying!). I knew the basic foundational principles on which she lives her life. The Holy Spirit does the same with us; it is within His personality to know our core values, and He often helps — if we are willing — to shape those values and beliefs.

Of course, our marriage wouldn't be a good marriage if I still only knew those core things. I have to get intimate and I have to know the silly things, as well. For example, if I could eat anywhere for dinner I would almost always choose a chain restaurant and order chicken tenders; however, my wife would want to go to the newest restaurant in the city to taste their flavors and better understand the food culture there.

The Holy Spirit's ways are similar to (and better than) this. If you get to know the Holy Spirit, you'll find He's not just interested in your theology but also in your personality also. This may sound funny, but often when I am driving alone, getting groceries or even just getting ready for the day I will talk to, laugh with and even joke with the Holy Spirit. Let me explain; in no way am I being disrespectful or kooky. I'm not turning to the empty passenger seat and trying to tell the Holy Spirit a knock-knock joke. Everyday I just decide to wake up with the assumption that God wants to get to know me, so I give Him that opportunity. By doing this I am experiencing the Holy Spirit's personality and intellect.

THE "FEELS" OF THE HOLY SPIRIT

One of the most common things I hear — and this isn't necessarily a bad thing — is that someone is "feeling something from the Holy Spirit..." People can feel the Holy Spirit but we mustn't forget that He feels us also. I once heard a preacher say, "If I don't feel God, I'm going to make sure He feels me."

I would venture to say that the Holy Spirit has a complete understanding of His own emotions, and has more perfectly expressed emotions than anyone here on earth.

Don't grieve God. Don't break his heart. His Holy Spirit, moving and breathing in you, is the most intimate part of your life, making you fit for himself. Don't take such a gift for granted.
Ephesians 4:30 MSG

Now I urge you, brethren, by our Lord Jesus Christ and by the love of the Spirit, to strive together with me in your prayers to God for me.
Romans 15:30 NASB

There are few things better than feeling the presence of God. I wonder if God feels the same way — that nothing is better than when He feels us? The two verses above describe the spectrum of emotions the Holy Spirit feels. Holy Spirit has a capacity to feel all emotions, as well as completely understand them.

The most important thing to remember about the Holy Spirit's emotions is that they are real and always present. If we were to live in a way that always pleases Him, we would probably have much healthier and more enjoyable lives.

THE WILL OF THE HOLY SPIRIT

I currently have a cat that has a will of his own, which is primarily just eating and sleeping. Often when people say a person or animal has a will of his own it's a negative attribution. However, when it comes to the Holy Spirit He most certainly has a will of His own! His will is the will of the Father. In no way is God's will a thing of negativity or annoyance if we are in right-standing relationship with Him. Our role in relationship with Him is not to simply observe His will, but to be obedient to it.

My wife and I have a sin habit, and that habit is called Waffle House. It should almost be a sin considering how good those waffles are in comparison to how dirty their floors are. So we frequent this 24-hour breakfast place all the time for quick bites to eat; one of our favorite things about it is that we can have it literally anytime, even Christmas morning if we wanted.

One morning we decided to go out for breakfast, or as my wife puts it, it was my "turn to cook". So Waffle House it was! We got a seat and began to order our food from our waitress, who was clearly not having a good day. She had been working two shifts and they had started early in the morning — the 1:00 a.m. kind of early. It was almost noon when we got there, and she still had many hours to go. We tried to make her laugh but it wasn't going over too well, so we stopped trying and just went about eating our food. Near the end of the meal I was getting frustrated with the service. That's when my wife, as usual, brought me down to earth and reminded me how hard our waitress was working. At that moment, Holy Spirit laid something so heavy on my mind. I can't tell you why, but for some reason the Holy Spirit really likes to heal people and this lady was next on His list.

The waitress came up with the check and my wife began to minister to her by verbally appreciating her service to us. The waitress's walls began to tear down as she opened up to us about some situations in her life. A thought kept coming to me for the next ten minutes as we talked. I have found that the Holy Spirit doesn't just gives words, but He has desires about timing as well. Just because I hear His voice doesn't mean I'm supposed to say anything right away. After a few more minutes, I could tell that I needed to speak up so I asked the lady if by any chance she was having problems with her back. She responded by laughing and confirmed what I had asked. Immediately she told us that there was no way she was going to get it fixed because it had been so long and the surgery would be too expensive.

Isn't it great that we have a God who isn't limited by our limitations? I asked permission for my wife and I to pray for her and she willingly threw out her hands for us to hold. I laughed and then began to pray. You see, when the Holy Spirit has a will He makes a way through our emotions, feelings and even our bad days. While we were praying, she began to explain how the pain was rapidly going away; she was quite shocked that after only a few seconds of praying her back was totally healed by the will of God.

I didn't decide to heal this woman — or anyone for that matter — for I don't decide when miracles happen. I am simply the vessel. If I try to conjure up some sort of will of my own, I will be relying on my own power. Spoiler alert: I have no power outside of God. If I were to make things up, I doubt that anything would happen. We must submit to the will of God in order for us to be a part of it.

CH 2 REFLECTION

PRAY THAT YOU WILL SEE HIS PERSONALITY

Everyday is now an opportunity for you to see the Holy Spirit's personality throughout your daily life. Start filtering events through the scope of what you can learn about God's personality through them, whether it is good or bad to you. God may cause you to see differently if you see His personality through the situation.

_____

_____

_____

_____

_____

_____

_____

_____

_____

THRÉÉ: HÉARINQ HIS VOICÉ

The voice of the Holy Spirit is as loud or as quiet as you make it. At a camp where my mentor was speaking and brought me along for, he spoke a message and it was particularly supernatural. It was the second or third night of the camp, and the services had been great with many people getting healed and filled with the Spirit. Before every service I am a part of I always pray for any last minute details the Holy Spirit wants to share with me. Often times He will give me something about a healing needing to take place or a general word for the congregation, but this time was different. This time I heard something I had never heard before.

I was pacing back and forth in the cabin in the middle of the afternoon desperate for God to speak about that night. I had already written down a couple of things that God had spoken to me to address: someone with a blind eye and someone with chronic back pain. All of a sudden God dropped a name in my mind. If I am completely honest, this hadn't happened to me before so I was very speculative about it, especially because we were as far north as you could get in America. But this name was as southern as they come; her name was Mary-Beth. It was one of those double first names so I was even more nervous about it, because out of all the people in the world very few have two first names. Nevertheless, I wrote it down and put the note with the healings and her name in my pocket.

The end of the service came and I joined my mentor on the stage to give a couple words to the people at the camp. I asked if there was anyone in the crowd struggling with a back problem and about ten people responded and were healed. I heard the Holy Spirit bring Mary-Beth to my attention. I tried to push the thought to the back of my mind, and asked for anyone who was struggling with sight to come forward if they were able. An elderly lady who'd lost sight in one of her eyes miraculously received sight again, but I wasn't excited at all because I knew the Holy Spirit was telling me over and over to mention Mary-Beth to the audience.

After having made the announcement for the people with the back and eye trouble, I somewhat joked with God that He'd better be right. I asked the crowd if the name Mary-Beth meant anything to anyone. I ended up praying for some other people, and near the very end of the night a lady came up to me with a young girl. Her name? Mary-Beth.

The woman began telling me how the night before — just under twenty-four hours prior — Mary-Beth's mom took her to a park and dropped her off telling her that she was done with her. Mary-Beth was only twelve years old. The lady telling me the story spoke of how she was driving and randomly saw the young girl in the park late at night and asked Mary-Beth if everything was okay. Long story short, she took Mary-Beth to camp for the week praying the situation would sort itself out while there.

I will be honest in telling you that I had no idea what to do so I just prayed, and as I was praying the Holy Spirit told me very directly to say something to this good Samaritan of a woman — something I would normally never say in a situation like this. I told her that God kept bringing the words 'foster parent' to my mind. The lady broke down crying, as she had been praying about that very thing that morning and what God spoke through me ended up confirming what she was supposed to do.

HEARING FROM GOD

In the Mary-Beth story God was giving me words of knowledge, which is when God tells you something that there would be no way of you knowing without Him telling you. For example, I didn't know there was a Mary-Beth in the crowd let alone a whole moment God wanted to have with her. However, God gave me that information supernaturally through the gift of words of knowledge.

I can tell you that this is not always what happens; whether it's a name or a sickness it doesn't always happen in that way. Hearing from God like that is a special event, but what is so amazing about God is that He wants to talk to us and hear us through the Holy Spirit.

There are two parts to hearing from God: you listening to what God is saying, and God listening to what you are saying. There is only one thing you need to do in order to hear what God is saying, and that is to listen. Listening is the act of trying to hear. The best way to hear from God is to put yourself in positions where you can listen to Him; over time this will become second nature and you'll realize that God is talking to you even when you're sleeping.

In the Bible there are countless stories where people hear from God in special events, and there are times when He speaks and no one hears Him. The very first thing in the Bible that was spoken by God was when He spoke, "Let there be light." No one had been created yet to hear that voice. However, everything is under the command of God's voice; therefore, there was light. God creates with His voice. When God commands, loves, shares, rebukes, punishes, convicts, empowers and supports — basically any other characteristic or verb that God does — He often speaks it. God most certainly speaks His mind.

In the Bible, and especially in the Old Testament, people audibly heard from God; they heard His actual voice. I have met only one person, and heard of only a few others, who God speaks to in this way and it's quite special. But that isn't necessarily normal. What's normal is found in the New Testament (which includes now) where we hear His still small voice to us during moments in our daily lives. The big question, though, is how?

Earlier I wrote of listening in order to hear, but I feel as if I should go into detail about this. Hearing from God is no longer a special event like it was in the Old Testament where only specific people heard from Him. So relieve yourself of all the pressure of trying to get God to talk to you. He could've already spoken to you through this very book. God speaks to us in a variety of ways.

THREE WAYS GOD SPEAKS TO US

1. THE BIBLE

God speaks to us in a variety of ways. First and most importantly, He speaks through His Word, also known as the Bible. If you want to hear from God in the next five seconds all you need to do is open up your Bible and start reading.

If you are by yourself while reading this I want you to fake a sneeze. For real... three...two...one...ACHOO. Okay, now after you fake a sneeze I want you to fake a breath...three...two...one... How was it? Did you fake a breath? Probably not because it is impossible to do so. You might make some noise, but that's impossible to do without air entering your lungs. Here's what I have found to be true: the Word of God is God-breathed, not God-sneezed.

All scripture is breathed out by God and profitable for teaching, for reproof, for correction, and for training in righteousness, that the man of God may be complete, equipped for every good work.
2 Timothy 3:16 ESV

Here's the thing about a breath: a breath is constant; it is needed for life and without it you aren't going to last very long. While a sneeze, on the other hand, is random; you can't control anything that is going on, and often times it makes a mess. The

40

Bible is like a breath. It should be a constant in our lives, because it will give us life for daily living.

The Bible is the best way to hear from God, and it is the foundation on knowing if you are hearing from God. All other ways of God speaking need to be filtered through the Word of God; this is also how you know you are hearing God speaking to you. When you question if God is talking to you, just examine what the Bible says. If it aligns with the Bible then it's most likely God talking to you.

I used to try to hear from God through the Bible by opening it up, flipping to a random verse and hoping that it was a word from God to me. The problem was that when I would land on a verse like this:

A certain young man was following him, wearing nothing but a linen cloth. They caught hold of him, but he left the linen cloth and ran off naked.
Mark 14:51-52 NRSV

You can clearly see why this method is silly, but I would recommend that you start reading the Bible on your own. More than likely the Bible will start to speak to you and you won't have to even try searching. You'll be blown away by how God can speak to you through His Word.

2. HIS VOICE

The second way God talks to us is through His Holy Spirit. As just mentioned, everything you hear — no matter how much you feel it or know that it's God — needs to be filtered through Scripture. The Holy Spirit is constantly talking to us on behalf of God the Father. The Bible even says in Romans 8:34 that Jesus is actually praying on our behalf. When you are praying to God you are activating your relationship with all aspects of God. You are praying to God through the Holy Spirit, who was made available for you through Jesus.

In my experience, hearing His voice is done in two main ways: through prayer and through thought. Everyone hears from God differently and uniquely. I hear from God most when I am praying and randomly when He brings something up in my thoughts, which also happens when I am praying. Hearing through prayer is quite simple. You just need to stop talking for a minute and listen to what God has to say. For me that usually means clearing my mind and telling God that I am listening, and within a couple of seconds I usually find myself thinking about something very specific and clearly from God. The more you pray the more you'll hear from God, and the more He'll hear from you.

The other way I often hear from God is what I like to call hearing God in the random. There is no specific place or time when I hear from God like this, but it often comes when I have in some way made myself available for God to speak. This can be when God is telling me to do something, or it can be Him showing me something that makes me laugh. The main venue when it comes to hearing from God is availability.

3. OTHER BELIEVERS

God speaks through His Word, His Spirit, and the third way that you and I can hear from Him is through other believers – His people. You shouldn't expect God to speak to you through people if you don't have Christian community. That couldn't be more true. The quickest way for you to silence God is to not read your Bible and to not be involved in Christian community. I will reiterate because of how important this is: no matter who it is in your community, whether it's a pastor, friend, parent or even spouse, you must filter what they say through the Bible if they are attempting to speak on His behalf. God's voice is rooted in the Word. Most of the time when you hear from Him, He will simply confirm what He has already spoken in the Word, but relate it to your life situation.

Therefore, as the Holy Spirit says, "Today, if you hear his voice, do not harden your hearts."
Hebrews 3:7-8 ESV

CH 3 REFLECTION

TAKE TIME TO LISTEN TO GOD

Everyday is an opportunity for you to hear from God. Make it a priority everyday to try to hear from God through His Word, His Spirit and His people.

ASK WHAT NOW?

Now that you will be hearing from God on a continual basis, the most important thing you can do once you hear from God is ask this simple question: What now God? Then let God speak. More often than not, God will keep speaking to you about what He initially spoke to you.

_____

_____

_____

_____

_____

_____

_____

FOUR: RELATIONSHIP WITH THE HOLY SPIRIT

Whenever I describe my relationship with the Holy Spirit I can only find one way to really define it. I know that not everyone has the maturity or masculinity to understand it, but it is the truth. The Holy Spirit is like a husband, but not in some bizarre or weird way. When I look at the traits the Bible says a husband should have, I find that the Holy Spirit has those attributes and takes on those roles for me — and everybody who lets Him. A husband should be a protector, provider, steward, communicator and leader of a family (as well as many other things). The Holy Spirit is to me what I am trying to be to my wife. If ever I need to know how to be a better husband, I honestly look at how the Holy Spirit treats me and seek to love my wife in similar ways.

I know that some people can't get over that last paragraph without thinking that I am out of my mind for saying such a thing, but let's get some better understanding. A relationship with the Holy Spirit isn't like any earthly relationship, friendship or even marriage; it's something far deeper and more intimate. On earth our relationships only last so many years, and I can only understand and know so much about a person. God has known me since forever and will know me forever; therefore, the relationship is eternally distinct.

So how on earth do we get a relationship with the Holy Spirit and not be strange about it? Well, I think the first thing is understanding that He already has a relationship with us. I have the awesome honor of being an older brother to two adopted siblings who were born in Haiti. They joined our family at pretty young ages, and the younger of the two — Armon — doesn't know much about his mom because of the length of time he spent in an orphanage. However, his mom knows exactly who he is. That's what some people have right now in regard to their relationship with the Holy Spirit. He knows you, but you may not really know Him. The greatest thing in this life is that we get to know Him and He will never reject us here on earth.

THREE WAYS TO HAVE A BETTER RELATIONSHIP WITH THE HOLY SPIRIT

1. TIME

Of course the idea of having a relationship with a deity sounds bizarre, and I get that; however, God isn't some deity. He is the creator of the universe and He actually decided to let us have relationship with Him. So how do we do this then? It is actually very similar to any relationship you have in that it gets better with time. That's the currency of this relationship, and I think it's what gets His attention more than anything. If God is outside of time and we let Him into our personal time, it in itself must be an amazing joy that God has when we let Him in.

We have limited time on earth, and the relationship we end with on earth is the relationship we begin with in Heaven. I don't see anywhere in Scripture where it says that we get to Heaven and all of a sudden we have a perfect relationship with God, and that's because every relationship's bonds are found in time. Make the most of it. I'm not saying you should spend every moment of your life praying, but every moment of your life should reflect your prayer life.

2. KILL THE COMPARISON

Comparing yourself to other friends

or pastors happens easily when you see the fruit of their relationships with the Holy Spirit. The root of a comparison in regard to a person's relationship with God is usually based off of works. You see someone pray for the sick and they're healed, or you have that friend who has never said a curse word in his entire life. Whatever it may be, stop. There is nothing that robs your life of joy more than comparison.

I have mentors in many areas of my life, whether that be ministerial, fitness, marriage and others. I can't compare myself up to their level, but I can come to their level through doing what others do. This is what makes a small group, church or community great; you inspire others and you in turn get inspired.

3. TAKE A RISK

In any relationship there is always some level of risk involved, whether you risk your pride asking someone who is way out of your league on a date, or even just seeing if someone wants to go watch a game with you. What I mean by taking a risk in this way is that you need to listen to what the Holy Spirit says. If He says He's going to heal someone then pray. If He nudges you to pay for someone's gas, do it. There is almost never a time when something can go wrong anyway. For example, let's talk about praying for the sick.

By now you should understand who the Holy Spirit is, and hopefully you are starting to hear His voice more. So let's say you're at the store and He nudges you to go pray for someone. You will never know the miracle you missed out on being a part of if you don't pray. On the other side of that, if you go over and the person doesn't get healed for some reason or just declines prayer, well...what harm was done? You aren't God so you can't control if someone will be open to prayer. There will be times when things don't work out for whatever reason. In those moments, though, all that does is show you that it isn't based off of your ability. When it does turn out the way you think it will next time, God will get that much more of the glory.

WHAT DOES THIS LOOK LIKE EVERY DAY?

When I was in college I went to a biblical studies university in Texas where I was an RA (resident assistant). At a normal college your job is to make sure people aren't dead from all of their drinking. At my school we were basically just making sure they weren't drinking or staying out past the school's curfew. The other unique aspect of being an RA at a Bible-based college is that you lead devotions once a week for your hall of guys or girls. Every week I would often come up with something to pray about with the guys, and we would wait on the Holy Spirit in the best way we knew was healthiest. This was the beginning of me learning to take risks.

God was doing something very unique during one devotion night. He told me to do something that no other hall was doing. In most of the other halls the RA would read a verse and talk about it, but since we were at a Bible college that was how we spent most of our days anyway. Instead, I decided to host prayer nights. On this particular night I felt strongly that I needed to trust what the Holy Spirit was telling me and take a risk. I am very much against anything weird, and this was certainly up there. As the Holy Spirit led me, I simply had the men pray while facing their doors in the hall. The Holy Spirit told me to go from guy to guy and pray whatever came to my mind. So I did, and to my surprise it worked. By the end of the forty-five minutes of prayer one person was baptized in the Holy Spirit, and almost everyone was given a word that was specifically for a situation they were involved with that very day.

When we step out and take risks, whether it's leading a devotional at work or inviting someone to church, the Holy Spirit will never intentionally embarrass you but He will stretch you. All He wants is relationship with us so that more people can have relationship with Him forever.

A relationship with the Holy Spirit can always get better and can begin at any time. Don't wait any longer if you feel like you don't have a relationship with the Holy

Spirit. Don't even finish this paragraph until you pray and let Him know that you are in! This doesn't have to be awkward or stressful; it just has to be authentic.

Think of your best friend. Have them in mind? Okay, what makes him or her your best friend? Is it that you both like the same things or that you just click? I cannot speak for you, but my closest friends are either those who I have spent the most time with or those I've had the best time with. In the most simplistic thinking, that's what a relationship is with the Holy Spirit. You are either spending time with Him, or you are having the best time with Him. The goal for everyone should be to have both consistency and quantity with the Holy Spirit. This could be as easy as waking up and reading your Bible before you take a shower every day. I promise that you will read your Bible and pray more if it is a prerequisite to taking a shower.

You also need authentic moments — those times of fasting or staying up and intentionally praying over your home or business and listening to the Holy Spirit with a notepad in hand to write down everything He says to you. The benefit is that often you will find yourself being a part of someone else's moment. As soon you have a relationship with the Holy Spirit, you will want to introduce Him to everyone you know. But you don't have to be awkward about it.

The Holy Spirit isn't weird. People, on

the other hand, are very weird. When people receive the Holy Spirit in their lives, He doesn't start doing crazy things with people. People do crazy things with the Holy Spirit! You'll realize that you have nothing to be afraid of once you understand that the Holy Spirit isn't weird. If you know the truth that He isn't weird and you don't make your interactions weird, then they won't be. This will set you up for the Holy Spirit to move in your life and impact others, because He'll be able to entrust you with those opportunities.

THREE WAYS TO MAKE SURE YOU AREN'T WEIRD

1. DON'T FAKE IT

The Holy Spirit is not your superpower; He's your God and friend. There is never a need to conjure anything, or make anything bigger than it already is with God. The worst thing that you can do is try to do things in your own ability. I have bad news. You have absolutely no power to heal the sick, ability to raise the dead or intelligence to know what is going on in someone's life without them telling you. You need the Holy Spirit to do all of that. Supernatural things are awesome, but they are only supernatural if God is doing them. Trust that God will use you when and how He wants. There's no need to make things up when you are waiting on God for your next assignment.

All these (supernatural gifts) are empowered by one and the same Spirit, who apportions to each one individually as he wills.
1 Corinthians 12:11 ESV

2. NO NEED TO PULL THE GOD CARD

One thing that can happen when you start to have a relationship with the Holy Spirit is that what you say may not really be what you're trying to say. For example, whenever someone starts telling me, "God is saying to you right now that..." I usually don't take them all that seriously. If you say things like that, people may find it very hard to take you seriously because you'll proba- bly be talking with a lot more authority than you actually have in that moment. There are times where people start conversations that way and the word they give is spot on. How- ever, if the newspaper gets delivered in the rain and I read it when it's wet, is it news? Yes, but it's the not the way I should be get- ting it because a newspaper isn't made to be wet when it's delivered. The best way to tell someone that you are hearing something or feeling a certain way is to be honest and say just that. "I feel like..." or "This could just be me but..." are the kinds of words that can really lower someone's guard and, more often than not, help someone receive what you're trying to deliver.

Always remember that you are not the mail; you are just the mailman. Let the Holy

Spirit work through you in such a way that you don't need credit, because it's not like you wrote the letter anyway.

3. BE YOURSELF

I will be the first to tell you that being yourself isn't the easiest thing when it comes to a relationship with the Holy Spirit. Let's be honest. If we see someone who appears to have it all together, we want his life or even his relationship with God. I look up to some pastors and preachers as both ministers and as people of God. I was once a part of a conference a couple years back, and I remember a man who referred to himself as a revivalist. I thought, "This is quite the title for a person to give himself," but he turned out to be as authentic as men of faith come. I saw how he heard from God, and that inspired me and has impacted how I minister to people to this day.

People are great examples, but they are terrible gods. I found myself being more amazed by this man of God, rather than the God who was in the man. Once I figured this out, I had a shift in thinking. I realized that instead of trying to be someone else that I need to be who God created me to be.

You may see preachers, friends, or videos of people praying and think that amazing things happen when they pray. I remember watching a video of someone praying for a people, and over time the people said they felt the power of God. The man ministering would say, "Double it, Lord!" As he continued to pray, to my amazement some would give an emotional response or even experience a miracle. Later, I found myself praying for someone, saying that phrase and nothing happened. For about three weeks, time and time again, I demanded that God double whatever He was doing. Once while praying for someone the Lord hit me with conviction. He showed me that when I try to be someone else I devalue the creation of God. This may seem like an odd example, but it had great significance to me. The experience showed me that I need to pray and minister to others in the way that God has gifted me. By doing so, I give Him the opportunity to use me and not some conjured up version of me.

A relationship with the Holy Spirit is not complicated or weird. It is what you make it and what you put into it. It is like every other relationship you have, but it just so happens that this friend refuses to give up on your friendship. Push yourself to make Him your friend and you will not denied. You will be empowered.

CH 4 REFLECTION

PRAY LIKE YOU ARE TALKING

This does not have to be your new way of praying by any means. But if you find yourself in a place where it still isn't fully feeling like you have a relationship with the Holy Spirit, simply try talking to Him. Begin to let Him know how you're feeling, then listen. I promise that will hear from Him if you listen.

_____

_____

_____

_____

_____

_____

_____

_____

_____

FIVE: KICK FEAR IN THE MOUTH

When I was seven years old I was on vacation with my family in Florida to do what most people do when vacationing there: go to Disney, get sunburned and eat far too much food. When our trip was over we had an early afternoon flight home. However, due to large storms our flight was delayed by over twelve hours and our plane changed three times.

By 2 a.m. a storm was still raging on, but we were finally able to board a plane. We glanced at our tickets and realized that one of us had to sit at the back of the plane near the engines and apart from the rest of the family. As a seven year old who wanted to prove his manhood, I decided this was the moment I would become a man. So I asked my mom if I could sit by a stranger. She couldn't have cared less after the events of the day; off I went down the terminal toward my seat and my manhood.

Up to that point in my life I had never seen a dead person, but for a good couple of minutes I thought I was sitting next to one. The lady next to me smelled like a mixture of your grandma's worst cooking and my actual grandmother. She didn't appear to be breathing, but as soon as the plane's loud engine started up she quickly arose in posture and immediately began telling me about how I looked like her grandson. At that point, I probably looked dead out of my seven-year-old boredom.

I must pause to bring up something that is quite heavy on my heart: seatbelts. Can we be real and admit that the seatbelts we put on in airplanes are about as useless as the "recliner" button. When was the last time you saw on the news that a plane crashed into the earth but the sole survivor happened to be the only one wearing a seatbelt? Yeah, that's right — never. Nonetheless, I still wear my seatbelt... Okay, back to the story.

So this is where the story gets good. The plane slid left and right as we gained speed on the runway, lifting off of the ground and coming back down multiple times as we began to take off. Finally our plane was in the air and we started the two-hour trip home to Michigan.

On a normal flight the pilot spends about ten to fifteen minutes getting to a cruising altitude of around thirty thousand feet. On our flight, at just around eight minutes into the flight is when the bad news began. As you can imagine, we were quite high in the sky at that point. The emergency lights (which are not very impressively lit for the occasion) came on without any warning, and it seemed like all of the other lights in the plane went off also. There was almost no illumination in the cabin except for the continuous flashes of lightning that could be seen through the countless plane windows.

You're probably thinking to yourself that this was a pretty rough situation; you are correct. And it got worse. The lights were basically off for about ten seconds, which is just enough time to imagine all the movie scenes you've seen where a plane crashes. After those ten seconds the power on the entire plane shut down. Remember, I was sitting right next to the engine where it is usually quite loud. The sound of it didn't just get quieter; the engine had completely turned off into silence.

The elderly lady who was sitting next to me decided to try to persuade me into believing that the wind was enough to make the plane glide all the way to Michigan. I may have been only seven at the time but I knew one thing: gliding is just another word for falling, and that's what we did. The engines didn't turn on for the rest of the flight. We tilted downward and went increasingly faster toward the runway we had taken off from just minutes prior.

As a seven year old I had probably prayed the salvation prayer a good 12,431 times, but this probably bumped it up to a good twenty thousand. All I can remember is that over the next couple of minutes I grabbed one of those mini pillows they used to pass out, shoved it into my face and kept praying, "JESUS, JESUS, JESUS!" The next thing I knew we landed, firefighters rushed from the back of the plane (I still have no idea how they got onboard), and we eventually got off and headed to a hotel room for the night only to try to catch another flight in the morning. We still didn't have a clue of what had actually gone wrong on our adventurous flight. I know what you're thinking. You read the part about firefighters and so far you haven't heard about the fire, but just hold tight. I'm getting there.

When we woke up the next morning in our hotel near the airport, we began talking about the events of the night before. I desperately tried to convince my parents that rather than spending just two hours flying home we should spend 12 hours driving instead. It didn't work. Right as my mom finished telling us to get ready to leave we saw on the TV that overnight a flight had made an emergency landing. We were blown away.

It didn't take long for us to realize that the news anchors weren't coincidentally talking about another flight. We looked at our tickets and compared them to the story being told, and the flight they were talking about was ours. According to the news, the plane had an electrical issue in the cockpit that ignited a small fire. It's not exactly what you'd think when you hear a plane was on fire but, nonetheless, it was technically true.

Needless to say, after that experience I wasn't a huge fan of flying. Many years later I was offered the opportunity to go with my dad on trips to New York, Chicago, Los Angeles — all places that we would have to fly to visit. My answer was always a quick "yes", but I had the condition that we should just drive the twenty-four or forty-eight plus hours to get to some of these vacations, But that wasn't really what my dad had in mind for a vacation. Obviously, those trips rarely happened and it was really quite ridiculous. My dad would have the whole trip planned out, the resources to pay for wherever we wanted to go and to do whatever we wanted to do. The intended goal for these trips was to bring us closer, yet I wouldn't go because of fear. My fear was keeping me from going the places my father wanted me to go.

Fear is the greatest tool the enemy uses in order to stop you from doing what God has called you to do. Fear is faith in something that probably won't happen. Miracles happen where there is no fear — only faith.

Jesus never told someone that their lack of fear healed them, but rather that their faith made them well! Fear is an all too real aspect of living a Spirit-filled life, especially when God tells you to do something that you have never done before.

Do you ever feel as if God is telling you to do something, then end up pacing around wherever you are trying to figure out if it's really God or just you? Or even worse, has your mind ever started racing with thoughts of what would happen if things didn't work out the way you thought they should? That used to be me every day of my life. I would often wake up in the mornings fearful that God would instruct me to do something, because I knew that I wouldn't do it unless I was 110 percent sure that it was going to work out. We have to take risks in order to have faith. The problem was that, like many people, I didn't like the idea of taking a risk and failing.

So how did I kick fear in the mouth? In all honesty, I got to a place where I no longer cared what other people thought of me. One day while praying I felt God convicting me in a way that was beyond any conviction I had ever experienced. I remember vividly God speaking to me through my thoughts, "If you believe I heal the sick, how much must you hate people if you don't pray for them?" God spoke that to me and it is what I think of every day that I wake up. If I see people who are obviously in pain or sick, how I must hate them if I choose not to pray for them.

I now live life unafraid of what people think. Rather, I am afraid of how long someone will be without faith if I don't share mine. So let's talk about some practical steps to kicking fear in the mouth.

HOW TO KICK FEAR IN THE MOUTH

First you have to stop caring what people who will never see you again think about you. Most often when God wants to speak through me, whether at a church service or in public, rarely do I see that person again after I pray for them. We need to get to a place of faith with God where we can logically understand that our faith isn't limited to who may remember us. If people have an authentic moment with God, then they aren't going to remember you anyway.

Secondly, you must be grounded in a faith community. Fear is usually caused by a lie or past event that wasn't supposed to happen. When we surround ourselves with people who are faithful it's nearly impossible to be fearful. It's really quite simple. If you wake up every day and pray that God fills you up to new understanding of Him and faith in what He will do, then there is no room for fear because you've already been faith-filled, which makes you faithful.

Finally, you have to face your fear if you want to get rid of it. If you're afraid to pray for someone, then step out there with someone who isn't afraid. If you are afraid of losing your job, read the part in the Bible that says the Lord orders the steps of the righteous. If you're afraid you won't get married, then go on a date. If you're afraid of Hell, then choose not to go there. Some of these are silly, but the best way to kick fear in the mouth is to kick fear in the mouth. If you silence the mouth you'll stop hearing the junk trying to get in your life to stop you from living it.

CH 5 REFLECTION

KICK FEAR IN THE MOUTH

Figure out what you are most afraid of in regard to your walk with God. Face that fear head-on by putting your face in the Word and spending time with Jesus. Fear is a waste of your time, so go kick it in the mouth and shut it up.

SIX: BAPTISM IN THE HOLY SPIRIT

The baptism in the Holy Spirit is the empowerment to do so that more people may know. It is essential to all believers who want to impact their world. Without it there is no newfound passion, no overflowing presence, and it is significantly more difficult to spread the news of Jesus. I know this subject may seem overwhelming or complicated, but I assure you that it is neither.

Jesus promised the baptism in the Holy Spirit both before and after He arose from the dead (Mark 16:17, Luke 24:49, Acts 1:8). Jesus even went as far as telling His disciples not to leave Jerusalem until they received this baptism (Acts: 1:4-5). One thing that should be understood before going any further is that this is a separate experience from salvation; they are not one and the same. Salvation is a transformational act, while Spirit baptism is an empowering event.

WHAT IS IT?

The baptism in the Holy Spirit is the empowerment to spread the Gospel. The word 'baptism' can be confusing because we usually think of being dunked in water when we think of baptism. The Bible actually describes three distinctly different baptisms.

1. BAPTISM INTO THE BODY

This kind of baptism is metaphorical and has nothing to do with water. We see it in the Bible in 1 Corinthians 12:13 where it speaks of a baptism into the Body of Christ. Becoming a part of the Body of Christ happens at the moment of salvation. It is called a baptism into the body because it represents both our conversion and joining other believers as the Body of Christ. In a sense, you are submerged into this new culture — a 'Kingdom culture' as some would describe it.

2. WATER BAPTISM

In the Great Commission (Matthew 28:18-20), Jesus instructs us as believers to baptize new followers of Jesus in water as the acknowledgement of who God is in their lives. This publicly and symbolically demonstrates God's washing away of our sins. This is the symbolic declaration of our faith; we step into the water as our old selves and out of the water as our new selves.

3. SPIRIT BAPTISM

The prophet Joel foretells of this baptism all the way back in the middle of the Old Testament. This verse is also referenced in Acts 2:17.

> "I will pour out My Spirit on all flesh; your sons and your daughters shall prophesy, your old men shall dream dreams, your young men shall see visions."
> Joel 2:28 NKJ

Similar to the baptism into the body, this baptism involves no water. However, it is a spiritual moment and brings the start of a deep relationship with the Holy Spirit. We see this in the Bible with Luke, who was the writer of the books of Luke and Acts. He made it clear that this should be an immediate next step after salvation.

Imagine a cup that is full of water to the brim; that's what our life is like when we get saved and the Holy Spirit comes to live within us. The baptism of the Holy Spirit is like when I grab a hose that has endless amounts of water and I put that hose into the cup of water. What happens? The water overflows onto everything it surrounds. This happens through the gifts of the Spirit, which is what the next chapter is all about. Spirit baptism gives the ability to be an extraordinarily better witness. The only reason you wouldn't want this is if you have no intention of leading anyone to Jesus, and if you really know Jesus you should already be doing this to some extent.

WHO CAN RECEIVE THIS?

Not everyone can receive the baptism in the Holy Spirit. There is one condition to receiving this empowerment from Heaven, and that is that you must have received salvation. That's it. You don't need to take a test or have a special degree. If you want to be a better witness and be used in supernatural ways to expand the Kingdom, then Spirit baptism is for you.

Recall the verse in Joel and Acts that said, "...I will pour out my spirit on ALL flesh..." God wasn't lying and that is truly the desire of Heaven: to see every man, woman and child receive this empowerment to go and be a better witness with signs and wonders following. Honestly, who wouldn't want the faith to pray for the sick or the passion to see this world saved and set free? There is not one Christian I have met that doesn't want that in life.

SPEAKING IN TONGUES

One thing that's important to understand is that the baptism in the Holy Spirit is not speaking in tongues. That is what happens after you receive the filling of the Holy Spirit. It is the initial physical evidence to show you that you have received the Holy Spirit. In other words, it's the receipt of the transaction that has just taken place. Now, to go to the store just to get a receipt would be silly; you go to the store for actual products. The baptism in the Holy Spirit is like going to the store but not having to purchase anything, because God wants you to have everything. His way of showing that you have everything is that receipt — speaking other tongues. There are two operations for speaking tongues; one is private and one is public, and both are incredibly powerful.

The first benefit (outside of knowing that you have been baptized in the Holy Spirit) is that you have a new prayer language. The same thing you spoke when He filled you develops and you begin to get more confident. If you listen, you will realize when you begin saying other things. Praying in English (or any known language) is powerful, but you are praying your own will toward God. This, of course, is not bad in any way; however, wouldn't it be nice to have God tell you what to pray? Do you ever begin praying and after a couple of minutes you have no idea what to pray next? Your prayer language is a language given to you by God, and it is your way of praying the perfect will of God. Great faith is required to do this. You have no idea what you're praying, but what you are praying is what God wants you to pray. Your prayer language is for your private use. Sometimes I use mine when I am praying one-on-one with someone for healing or for them to receive Holy Spirit baptism, but I am never to just get on a microphone and start speaking it. Paul actually talks about this in 1 Corinthians 14 if you want to go deeper in understanding this.

The second benefit is for the body of Christ. Notice that there are no instances where you are to pray in the Spirit around unbelievers, because they will likely have no idea what is going on. The second benefit is actually a gift of the Spirit for which everyone should pray and seek. You will usually experience this in some sort of church service or gathering of believers, often during worship or prayer, when God will speak through someone in prayer language. Remember, God doesn't move people's mouths; He moves on their hearts. This is always accompanied by an interpretation of tongues, which is also a gift of the Holy Spirit. In short, interpretation of tongues can be described as God speaking through someone in an unknown language and giving someone else the ability to translate it so that the believers can be edified in their faith. You will know that the message is of God if what they say aligns with His Word and is loving.

HOW DO I GET THIS?

I was baptized in the Holy Spirit when I was in sixth grade and, to be honest, I had little idea of what happened and didn't do anything with it. To be completely honest, when I got back from that camp I was sure that God had given me the ability to run faster and that's what I thought the gifts were. Of course that wasn't true and is quite hilarious now, but that is not what I want you or anyone to experience.

The Baptism in the Holy Spirit is the ability to be a witness. In all honesty, if you aren't witnessing to people, then you don't need it. But if you want everyone you know and everyone you will know to know Jesus, then you need it. If you want to pray for the sick or to be used for any of the gifts of the Spirit, you need this.

If you have a relationship with Jesus and want His empowerment and a deeper relationship, then there is only one thing you need in order to be baptized in the Holy Spirit — faith. You can be filled with the Holy Spirit even as you read this book. It doesn't take a loud worship set or a special preacher or pastor praying for you to receive the baptism. This isn't about anyone or anything else besides you and God. All you have to do is get into a place where you best receive from God, whether that's in your car, at your church or even sitting in bed. Get into a position of receiving from Jesus and just begin to worship Him and tell Him that you want to be baptized. I believe that anyone who earnestly desires Spirit baptism and has faith that God will give it will be all set.

Once you have told God your heart and are ready to receive, do just that. Receive. Let God flow through you and do a work inside of you. You will know that you have received once you start speaking in other tongues. This is a language given by God in which you pray the perfect will of the Father. This is your receipt from this heavenly transaction. Relax and let God do the rest. He won't move your tongue for you, but just step out whenever you feel something different or have even one syllable in your mind. The best thing you can do is try, and God will not disappoint. The Bible clearly says that God wants to do this for you.

The baptism in the Holy Spirit changed my life. Unfortunately, daily life didn't change much until years after I was filled, but that was on me and not on God. I had so much fear and doubt about what God could do, but now I look back and wonder how many people could've been impacted if I would have let God have a deeper impact on me. Every day is an exciting journey; I wake up and wonder what awesome thing the Holy Spirit wants to do to and through me.

Once I got married the excitement multiplied, because my wife is also used in the workings of God but in different ways. This experience is not meant to be private, but it is personal. I tell my wife and closest friends what God is doing so that I stay accountable and never try to do things on my own, and so that others may be inspired to push themselves in their faith. The result is a small community of friends pushing one another and supporting a greater work than what is just happening within us.

CH 6 REFLECTION

WHAT IS SOMETHING YOU DO WITHOUT THE HOLY SPIRIT?

Figure out what are the things in life that you have been doing without the Holy Spirit. List them out and find ways to invite Him into those areas of your life. This may seem silly at first, but things like your finances or how you spend your spare time are things that are important to the Holy Spirit. He genuinely wants to make your life better with Him!

_____

_____

_____

_____

_____

_____

_____

_____

_____

SÉVÉN: GIFTS OF THE HOLY SPIRIT

At the beginning of this book I told a story about when the Holy Spirit used me in giving a young lady a word of knowledge about her physical pain, and then God subsequently healing her stomach and back instantly. This is normal.

If someone gave you a gift on your birthday, would you ever think of paying him back for it? Of course not, because you expect to receive gifts when it's your birthday. When you are filled with the Holy Spirit, every day becomes your birthday and someone else's quite often. See, the thing about these gifts is that they aren't just for you; they are for everyone. The Holy Spirit may use you to do something for someone else, but that's how multiple people get the same gift. I think most people are this way, but I personally think that on Christmas day it's just as fun, if not more, to give gifts than to receive them. The Holy Spirit gives out His gifts when and to whom He desires, but when we position ourselves to be used He uses us quite frequently.

There are actually nine distinct gifts listed in the Bible:

God's various ministries are carried out everywhere; but they all originate in God's Spirit. God's various expressions of power are in action everywhere; but God himself is behind it all. Each person is given something to do that shows who God is: Everyone gets in on it, everyone benefits. All kinds of things are handed out by the Spirit, and to all kinds of people! The variety is wonderful:

words of wisdom
words of knowledge
great faith
healing
miraculous acts
prophecy
discerning between spirits
tongues
interpretation of tongues.

All these gifts have a common origin, but are handed out one by one by the one Spirit of God. He decides who gets what, and when.

1 Corinthians 12:4-11 MSG

One thing to understand is that most

of these things can be done by anyone who has been filled with the Spirit. But there is a side of this where favor and anointing come into play, in which certain people operate in certain gifts in an extravagant way. That is seen throughout the Bible and throughout our world.

A long list like this can be overwhelming to think about or process, let alone reading some of these and not understanding what they even are. So for our sanity, let's break them down.

WORDS OF WISDOM

When you think of words of wisdom you may think of an old professor who sits back in his chair and begins ranting about all that he knows about astrophysics. This isn't that or some kind of parent trying to give you some motivation talk so you behave better. This is when someone would have no way of knowing what to do or say about a situation, but God supernaturally gives the person insight and the ability to speak into it. This can happen in counsel, conversation or even decision making. Receiving words of wisdom is probably the most natural gift out of the nine, and I would even argue that many people are used by the Spirit in this way and don't even know it.

WORDS OF KNOWLEDGE

This is where it started for me. Words of knowledge seem to come quite naturally to me in many situations. I can't explain why, but this is certainly where God began building my faith and training me. A word of knowledge is when God tells you something that you didn't already know. In the story about the woman in the beginning of the book, my hearing from the Holy Spirit about her stomach and back and telling her was a word of knowledge experience. They happen when we have no way of knowing information, but God does and He lets us in.

I recall the first time this happened. I was speaking in front of a small group of twenty people, and as the end of my message drew near I felt as if God was telling me to have everyone stand up and to pray for each of them. As I prayed for them, things came to my mind and I prayed them out. The people began to freak out at what I was saying. For every person who was there, God moved through me in a way where I didn't just speak up about a situation; I spoke to it. God empowered me in a very natural and level place. To be honest, I didn't feel like I was doing anything special. Like any other time I would pray, I was just praying what came to my mind.

As my faith grew I realized that God was going to use this gift in even greater ways. It is often used to build faith either because it proves that God is with us and knows what's going on in our lives, or it builds faith to what's about to happen. This happens quite often for me now, both in services and out in public. The story I told about the twenty people was God showing them that He was in the situation, but often God takes it another step further.

You may have noticed from previous stories in this book that most have begun with God telling me of something that a person hadn't yet told me. This is what I like to call the jumpstart. A jumpstart is where God speaks through us in order to build our faith and the faith of the one we are ministering to so that a greater work can be done.

There are moments with the Holy Spirit that are indescribably fun, like when you get to pray for a friend and they are healed. Once I was at a young adult service that I attended regularly and noticed my wife's friend before the service started. I went over to her and began some small talk. The words of knowledge hit me like a train, and it was undeniable that the Holy Spirit was trying to get my attention. She took a breath between sentences and I stole the conversation from her. Seemingly out of nowhere, I asked if she or someone in her family had been struggling with back issues for six years. She flipped out and told me that she was the one with the back pain. After the service my wife and I prayed for her and she was ecstatic! She was blown away that God would use someone, and she began to tell us how much it meant to her that God saw her issue. She was instantly healed of all back pain and hasn't experienced any since.

This is obviously not some ability I have. I almost failed anatomy in high school, and there's no way for me to know the things that God knows. This isn't some weird trick, superpower or extrasensory perception (ESP). The Holy Spirit gives words of knowledge. The best way to be used in this way is to simply tell God that you are open to being used in this way. The Bible says that we should earnestly seek and covet the gifts of the Spirit, so let him know. You have nothing to lose.

GREAT FAITH

The spiritual gift of faith is not to be confused with the idea of faith that saves, or saving faith. Every Christian has been given saving faith through Jesus Christ (Ephesians 2:8-9), but not all receive the gift of faith. The word 'faith' carries the notion of assurance in what can happen on the other side of faith. Those with this gift trust and confide in God, which allows them to live boldly.

The Bible tells us that the gift of faith is often accompanied by great works. This gift can be seen in action in Acts 3 when Peter sees a lame man at 'the Beautiful Gate' and calls on him to stand up and walk. Throughout the gospels, and throughout the Bible as a whole, we are able to see that faith starts more than just miracles; it can start movements.

This is a gift that is far too overlooked, but it is the gift that I ask for the most. Thirteen of the seventeen recorded healing instances Jesus performed in the Bible happened because of the person's faith. Jesus would often say things like, "Your faith has made you well." The operation of the other gifts is impossible without faith, so with great faith great things can happen.

During one service I prayed a for wonderful lady who was in her late eighties after I'd asked if anyone was struggling with their sight. I saw her raise her hand but she never came to the front where we were praying for people. After the service she was still sitting in her seat, so I walked over to her and asked if there was anything that I could pray for with her. Her response was so funny to me; she told me that I could pray for her, but that nothing was going to happen. As she said this, her friends sitting around her rolled their eyes; they all believed that she would receive her sight again.

At that moment I wasn't feeling a whole lot — not that I ever really do, but this was a big one to me. In my mind, the thought of a blind person getting back their sight took more faith than other things, which isn't true but it was certainly how I felt. While her friends and I began to pray, I was amazed at how quickly she started getting her vision again. God showed up and gave her some of her vision; it didn't come back completely that night but I believe that God moved in a mighty way over that woman.

Faith is a funny thing because it is belief in things that are not yet seen. Fear is the same; it is belief in something that has not yet occurred and being afraid that it will. Fear is just misplaced faith, and when praying for people we can often have our faith in the wrong thing. We can believe that there is no way God will do whatever it is that we're asking. However, what I have seen in the Bible and in my life is that nothing is impossible for those who have faith. Great faith is certainly a blessed gift.

HEALING

One day God put something in my heart and asked me how much I have to hate someone not to pray for them. I believe that God heals the sick, so as much as I can I offer to pray for the sick; I ask everyone how they are feeling. I have learned that for some reason people, even those who don't know me, are open to talking about their pain. Many times they will talk about it without even being asked.

After an incredible young adult service, I remember my wife and I walking up to a young lady who was just a couple years older than I was. She looked at me as if she had seen a ghost as I began to tell her the specific details the Holy Spirit had spoken to me about her physical limitations and pain. She had never seen or heard of anything like this. I first told her what I believed the Holy Spirit was telling me about her stomach issues, and that's when she gave me that look — she looked as if I had just secretly read her mind. She began to weep uncontrollably to the point where she had to walk away in order to regain her composure.

To say she was surprised would be a great understatement. After all, I was a complete stranger who'd just told her about her own pain; she hadn't told anyone except her doctor about it. After she got out of the momentary shock, she then told us how her stomach had been hurting on a constant basis for years. Even at that moment she was in great pain. I began to normalize the situation by letting her know that what was happening is completely normal and was purely the love of God.

After making sure it was okay, we began to pray for her and immediately the Holy Spirit spoke again. I asked her if she'd recently been in a car accident that injured her lower back. She told us that she had been in an accident, and that she had bulging discs in her back that were causing severe pain. She began to tell my wife and I that she had never felt anything like what she was feeling in that moment. Never had anyone told her what she hadn't told anyone else. She had never felt the presence of God, and she was having her first encounter with Him in a very bold way!

She explained in detail how God's promptings were so right. She had a stomach issue that couldn't be cured medically. I politely asked if my wife and I could continue praying for her. She was fully on board so we laid hands on her and began to pray again, believing for God to finish the work He had already started with the promptings of information He had given me (the Bible calls these promptings "Words of Knowledge").

She cried even more than before (which I didn't think was possible). She could hardly stand up straight, as it seemed as if all of Heaven was trying to force its way onto her. After just a minute or so I asked her what God was doing, and she exclaimed that where we'd placed our hands was burning hot. She even asked to see our hands to make sure nothing was on them. (I never personally feel heat when praying for someone, but this is not uncommon at all. God often does these sorts of things as a sign of His love and to show that He is working in a person's pain or issue.)

We prayed once again, then tested what God was doing with great faith. I asked her if she would be willing to move her back from side to side. She gave me a fearful look as she reluctantly tried. She moved her back from side to side, and excitedly exclaimed that God had put the disc back in place! She suddenly seemed even more surprised, as she had completely forgotten about her stomach pain; it was also gone! In just a matter of minutes, the young lady went from never knowing Jesus to being touched by Him in a miraculous way. The disc was put back as it should be, and her stomach was completely healed after years of pain.

She was a 25-year-old on a college campus, and had never before experienced God. She didn't ask for any of this. God had to specifically tell me to walk over to her and start the conversation. That's the God that I serve; that's just who He is. It doesn't matter where we are or what we've done, or even what prior experience we've had, God is relentlessly pursuing us to the point of using other people to get our attention.

Healing is something you can read in the Bible and that you can read of today. That's because Jesus is the same yesterday, today and tomorrow (Hebrews 13:8). We have a God who loves to heal the sick, and He also loves to give people the ability to do so in His power. His love of healing comes from the mere fact that He loves people.

At another time I prayed for someone who was keeping her medical issues pretty private. I knew her, but I had no idea what was going on with her. All I knew was that she was extremely sick and that she wanted me to pray for her. This was by far one of the coolest healings I have experienced because of how much faith there was going into it. There was an altar call at a service we were both attending; when she came up to me we were both incredibly expectant of what God was about to do. As I began to pray for her, I felt God tell me about where she was in pain and what was going on. I told her that I didn't know what was wrong with her, but then proceeded to tell her that God was giving me a word of knowledge about it. I told her that I felt as though the doctors didn't know exactly what it was, but that it was some sort of extreme fibromyalgia and that there was constant pain. She told me that was accurate and that there were a couple of other things along with that pain.

God telling me what was wrong with her wasn't a magic trick or to make her "feel good"; it was God showing both of us that He knew what was going on and that He sees our situations. Our already high amount of faith for this situation increased. I began to pray and as I started the power of God fell in a inordinate manner. I mentioned earlier in the book that I typically don't feel anything when I pray for someone, but this was different. It was as if I was hit with electricity from the top of my head and through my arms and hands as I prayed for her. She clearly felt it also because she nearly fell over multiple times. The presence and power of God was intense. This is not always the case, but when it is I see it as God just giving us a little extra dosage of power and showing us that He is clearly there and on our side.

What was very beautiful about this moment was that God wasn't done yet. Near the end of the time we had praying, God spoke a couple of other things to me that I shared. She confirmed it, so we prayed for that too. My friend was healed that day, and God's power was made known to those of us who were there. This healing happened in person, but God can do incredible things even if the person isn't in the room. Our God is omnipresent (He is everywhere at all times).

I was praying for healing over the entire crowd at a young adult service once, and one thing that I prayed was that God would heal backs even if that meant melting metal. I have no idea where that idea came from, so I was very obviously prompted by the Holy Spirit. The response was incredible; many people were healed of incurable issues. A man approached me later and he was holding his phone. He told me that he'd recorded me praying and sent it to his mom. I thought this was a little odd initially, but what He told me next astounded me. He informed me that his mom had been bedridden for the last twenty years. She had a metal rod up her back so she was completely unable to move her back or neck, which caused her a lot of pain. His mom called while we were talking to tell him that she was feeling better, and asked if I would pray for her. I took the phone to talk to and pray over her.

Within about thirty seconds she told me that could move her back and neck for the first time in twenty years. God healed a woman who had been in bed for twenty years.

God is bigger than anything we expect and always surpasses our expectations. The power of God is not something to be made up or exaggerated. It is by far the realest thing on this earth, and God wants to use His people to heal the sick — both believers and non-believers alike. In my eyes, healing is the greatest way to get someone to Jesus. When someone receives a gift like that from God, they understand that the giver is real.

MIRACULOUS ACTS

The gift of miracles is mentioned similarly to the gift of healing in Scripture. Often it seems that healing is what seems to occur in miraculous moments, but it is usually grander. Things like people being raised from the dead (yes, this still happens), people growing back limbs, and people getting out of wheelchairs are healings that are of miraculous power.

Those who operate with this spiritual gift usually have a heightened sensitivity to the presence and power of God through the Holy Spirit. They often have a special measure of faith and desire for God to reveal Himself and draw many to faith in His Son, Jesus Christ. The objective of every gift of the Spirit is for more people to know Jesus.

In my mind, miraculous acts are like the big red button of the spiritual gifts. They are when things really go down — those moments when people are left speechless and begin to live differently after seeing such things.

We know that Jesus performed many miracles during His earthly ministry, even more than those recorded in Scripture (John 20:30-31, Acts 2:22). The apostles regularly performed miracles of all kinds, including casting out demons, healings, raising people from the dead, striking people dead, causing blindness, and much more (Acts 2:43; 3:1-10; 5:1-16; 9:36-43; 13:4-12; 19:11-12). God wants to do much of the same through us. He loves to use His disciples, and we are to live as His disciples every day.

PROPHECY

The gift of prophecy is unique in that after Paul (the writer of many books in the New Testament) listed out the nine gifts, he then says in 1 Corinthians 14:1 that we should "pursue love, and earnestly desire the spiritual gifts, especially that you may prophesy." That out of all the gifts he singles out this one is so interesting to me. He didn't specify healing, miracles or even faith, but prophecy.

The word for prophecy used most often in the Bible is best defined as the ability to receive a God inspired word that is passed to others in the body of Christ. These words do not constitute the authoritative Word of God, but are the human interpretation of the word that was received. I mentioned in a previous chapter that we are not the mail; we are just the mail carriers of the Good News. Just because we might have said something of God doesn't make us any more holy, but I do believe it gives us a better relationship with God. If we steward His gifts well He is bound to use us more often.

I have been given many prophetic words, and about half either haven't yet happened or may never happen. If someone comes to you saying they have a word or prophecy from God for you and it aligns with the Bible, the absolute best thing for you to do is just to metaphorically stick that word in your back pocket. If it comes to pass, then you can take it out of your pocket and thank Jesus for the confirmation.

Sometimes it's obvious when it's not God, like the time I had someone call me telling me that God told them I was supposed to be a part of their weight loss pill pyramid scheme...yeah, I think not. But there are also times when the word can be God, and I just have to wait for it to happen. Something like that happened when I was a high school student at camp. A woman approached me and said, "Don't be afraid of her," and then she just left. I have no idea to this day who her is, or if the message was even from God. So I told myself not to think about it, and that if

God brought it back up in my prayer time or in a life situation then I'd have that moment to look back on as confirmation.

The best times are when you know what you've heard is from the Lord and Scripture supports it. One such time occurred when a friend and I met up to have lunch when I was in college in Texas. While we were eating some of Texas' best deep fried chicken, a lady and her husband came up to us and started speaking to us. We had actually known her as someone who attended the church where my friend and I served, so nothing seemed all that strange at first. She was very polite as we casually talked, then out of nowhere she asked quite kindly if she could pray over both of us. Let me remind you that we were in the middle of a chicken restaurant that was filled with enough people for things to feel a little awkward. I believe, though, that you must get past a little bit of awkward in order to get to a whole lot of awesome. So we were willing let her pray for us thinking the prayer would last only about ten seconds. Well, it ended up lasting about ten minutes. She told my friend some encouraging words about some life situations he was dealing with, and he later told me that they were spot on. Then the lady started praying for me.

Let's take a step back. At the time, I did graphic design in my spare time to make some income while in college. I would often think and pray to God asking when my work as a designer would stop, and if I would soon get into full time vocational ministry. When the lady at the chicken restaurant began prophetically praying over me, she said that I would not do graphic design forever and that it was just my work for a season. I had never told her what my job was, and there was no chance that she was able to figure it out. God was speaking through her. She went on to tell me that God had me right where He wanted me, and that I would do the things He told me to do when I received my calling to be an evangelist while in the sixth grade. My mind was pretty blown away by how much God was letting this acquaintance know about me, but that wasn't the end of what He wanted to tell me. The lady then prophesied that I would pray for the sick and they would be made well, and that she then had a vision of me laying my hand on someone's back and it was instantly realigned and healed.

The word was clearly from God firstly because of everything she said about me that she wouldn't have known was true. Secondly, everything aligned with God's Word. Lastly, all of those things have now come to pass as I'm writing this. I can't explain why, but many of my friends who are also used in healings seem to have greater faith for certain things. Another way to put it is that some people are used to heal some ailments more often than others. Every time one friend of mine prays for the deaf, they are then able to hear. A mentor of mine says that his ministry has seen a lot of knees get healed pretty easily. We all see a lot, but those are things that seem to come naturally for some. I just so happen to have seen more backs healed than anything else.

The prophetic word I was given was made whole at a camp one summer where I was praying for a lady who had scoliosis. Scoliosis can be treated but cannot be cured, and even the treatments involve the person being in almost constant pain. The woman told me that her back had been misaligned throughout her entire life. She was in her early twenties and about to get married, and she was quite hopeful that she would be healed. After politely asking permission, I put my hand on the top of her back and started praying. As I prayed, her spine began to move into place. I asked her to twist from side to side and to try to touch her toes. Then she screamed! She was able to do everything I'd asked. She told me that God supernaturally realigned her back and cured something that the doctors said was incurable. Not only did He do all of that, but the prophecy given to me at the chicken restaurant in Waxahachie, Texas, was fulfilled.

I didn't go chasing the fulfillment of the word and neither should you. Prophetic words will naturally come, and they will supernaturally edify us once they happen if they are biblical and of God.

DISCERNING BETWEEN SPIRITS

The biblical word for discernment describes being able to distinguish, discern, judge or appraise a person, statement, situation, or environment. The New Testament describes the ability to distinguish between spirits as in 1 Corinthians 12:10, and to discern good and evil as in Hebrews 5:14. The Holy Spirit will give discernment to show us if something is of God, or if something is demonic. This gift is useful in not being led astray by false teaching or getting involved with anything demonic.

Discernment is something that I personally do not operate in very often, and that's totally fine. I have to understand that the Holy Spirit gives His gifts out to whom and when He chooses. However, sometimes the Holy Spirit will let me know if someone is being oppressed or is possessed by something demonic. If that's the case, I deal with it in the biblical way of rebuke and let Jesus take over the situation.

Demons are most certainly real and there is no shortage of them on the earth, but there is no need to fear them. We have greater authority over demons when we are in relationship with Jesus.

TONGUES

We discussed this a good bit in the chapter on the baptism of the Holy Spirit, but there is a lot we can learn about it. Remember that the prayer language of tongues is the initial evidence of receiving the baptism of the Holy Spirit, and anyone who is filled with the Spirit can pray in tongues in their personal relationship with God. The gift of tongues is different, yet the same. It's not a different level or language of tongues; it's just a different operation of it. Praying in tongues is a faithful act of submission to God's authority in which we pray His perfect will through our prayers. A simple way of looking at it is that it's God praying through us what He wants us to pray. He doesn't move our mouths for us, but he moves our hearts toward Him.

The gift of speaking in tongues is for the edification of the church. When to do this is regarded in 1 Corinthians 14. In essence, it is for believers. To start speaking in tongues to someone who isn't a believer would be silly, because they wouldn't know what I'm saying and neither would I. The most common operation of this gift is when someone speaks during worship, or a time when God wants to speak to His people and someone is be moved to do so. Then the interpretation comes.

INTERPRETATION OF TONGUES

This goes hand-in-hand with tongues because it is dependent on someone being used in that gifting. I have seen where someone does both, but most often it seems as though God uses two people for this. So let's say your in a worship service and someone gives a tongue. The next thing you should hear is someone giving an interpretation of that tongue in the language of the people in the gathering. The interpretation will always be edifying and loving. If there is no love, then it is not of God because God is love. Everything He does is a sign or act of His love.

WHEN WILL GOD USE ME?

The operation of the gifts of the Spirit is something to be determined by the Holy Spirit. However, once you understand that He uses you in a particular way, or uses you often in one gifting, then let your relationship with the Holy Spirit guide that. Remember, you and the Holy Spirit have a relationship and you can ask Him at anytime what to do, or what He wants to do. The best question I can think to ask the Holy Spirit is, "What now?" That question allows me to position myself to hear His voice, and lets Him know that I am willing and faithful to do whatever He should ask of me.

Do not be discouraged if God isn't using you in the gifting you want. These gifts aren't superpowers. Just because one day someone isn't healed or set free doesn't mean that you won't ever be used in those gifts.

The best thing you can do every day when you wake up is to let the Holy Spirit know that you are willing and able to be used by Him. This is all a part of a relationship with Him; He wants to baptize you in His Spirit, save you from your sins and to use you in His gifts. Remember, though, that these are gifts so you should treat them as such. Be loving in everything you do and God will continue to use you mightily!

CH 7 REFLECTION

LET HIM KNOW THAT YOU ARE ON BOARD!
The Holy Spirit wants to equip you to be used in His gifts so that people may know Jesus. Let Him know that you are on board and ready for whatever He wants. If you ever get a hunch, a feeling or even a thought of ministering to someone in any way, ask the Holy Spirit and He will guide you. The worst thing that can happen is someone will say, "No.". Sometimes that will happen. We will be wrong at times, but all that does is remind us that God's ability is at work and not our own. If you see someone or know someone who is sick, pray for them. If you get a word for someone, give it. He wants to use you, so let Him!

_____

_____

_____

_____

_____

_____

EIGHT: YOUR FIRST MIRACLE

Miracles are like Heaven on earth. They are a glimpse of what Heaven will be — the restoration of mankind and intimacy with God. Miracles show people God's love to get them to God's love. Hopefully you have a better idea of who the Holy Spirit is, and know that you can and should have relationship with Him. Now that you have a basic understanding of His gifts, you are more than eligible to be used in the miraculous. Remember that this is what God does through us to people, and not us doing whatever we want in hopes that God shows up and creates a miracle. We don't need to ask God to bless what we're doing. If we wake up everyday asking God what He wants and we do that, it's already blessed because it's from God.

I know that the idea of praying for the sick or operating in any gift of the Spirit can make anyone nervous. I totally get that and have been there. The first time that the Holy Spirit ever used me to heal someone was when I was twenty-two years old. Don't think that if you're older that you're behind; remember, I went twenty-two years never doing this, but through Jesus I now do it all the time. The Holy Spirit wants to use everyone at any age and in any season.

The first time I prayed for and actually witnessed someone get healed was at the church where my wife led as a worship pastor in Atlanta, Georgia. The church held a teaching series about healing, and it was by far one of the best teachings I had ever heard on it. During the last session there were hundreds of people waiting to be prayed over for healing. I watched as some people wept, while others danced and laughed because of what God was doing in that place and in their bodies. I soon realized that there were far too many people to be prayed for in order for the session to end anytime soon. I saw that the prayer leaders were getting overwhelmed at the response, which is a good issue to have, but still an issue nonetheless. So my journey to my first miracle began. God spoke.

GOD SPEAKS

As I sat in my chair with the realization that the need for more people to pray for the sick was great, God spoke to me. God's voice is different to everyone so you need to figure out for yourself what it sounds like to you. It often comes to me as a thought, or a thought accompanied by a feeling. I find it hard to describe what it feels like, but when the Holy Spirit is speaking I just sort of know.

I'd prayed for people who were sick in the past, but I'd honestly never had them say they were better — especially not instantly. The longer I sat in that chair the more nervous I became. The what-ifs kept coming to mind. What if they aren't healed? What if I don't know what to pray? These are lies that the enemy puts in our minds to hold us back from God's plan. So I punched fear in the mouth, stood up, and went to the sick.

YOU MOVE

The hardest thing about God pushing us is that He often pushes us outside of our comfort zones into His comfort zone. Let's say you've heard from God, or at least you think you have, and you have a small seed of faith.

Now is your time to move and position yourself for a miracle. In my case, my next move was getting up from my seat, going to the authority in the room to get permission to pray for people, and then heading to the altar where people were lined up to be prayed over. Whatever your move turns out to be can look differently. The important thing is that you move out of your seat — your comfort zone — or even make the call to meet with someone. You need to go where the Holy Spirit tells you to go. As you read this, my hope is that the Holy Spirit starts bringing people up to your thoughts so you can pray for them.

The word I use is 'move'. However, all I mean to say is that you need to position yourself by talking to the person you feel you need to pray for, and sometimes they may just come to you. This is why you need to wake up and position yourself to hear from the Holy Spirit. He won't let you down.

THEY BELIEVE

The best thing you can do when praying for someone who is sick is to let go and let the Holy Spirit take over. I don't mean you don't say anything until you know the exact sentence; I just mean to be yourself and to pray like you would if you were in the car by yourself. Be you because that's the person God called to help perform the miracle. The next thing to do is encourage the person you're praying for. After you feel like God may have done something, test it out. If their knee hurt when they moved it, have them try and move their knee after you pray. You have nothing to lose. You aren't going to be the one healing them; Jesus will do the healing. You just be you. Pray and believe that Jesus will do it.

I believe that if you hear from God, move toward the action and believe that it can happen, God will use you in a mighty way to change the world around you. Soon you may find yourself asking everyone around you if they are sick, hurting or just need prayer. Jesus won't let you down, so don't give up if it doesn't work out the first or second or ten thousandth time. All it takes is one.

Let's get back to the story of my first time praying for someone to get healed. I was standing at the altar and a woman came up to me complaining about her hip. Her hip had been out of place for seven years, and she hadn't been able to run or walk without a limp. I prayed and gave it everything I had, and then I asked her how it felt. She told me it didn't feel any differently. So I gave it one more shot. I got down on my knees to place my hand on her knee, told God that I couldn't heal her but that He could, and asked that He would.

I stood up and asked the lady how it felt again, but there was still no change. I told her to keep praying, and she took one step. Within about half a second she began to weep uncontrollably. See, in order for her to know that she was healed she had to take that step of faith. God healed her and she was able to run and jump with ease.

HOW TO PRAY FOR THE SICK

One of the topics we get asked questions about the most, and receive the most requests to teach, is how to pray for the sick. I touched on it a bunch in this chapter, but I want to give a practical and simple outline of how we can do this in the most biblical and simple way.

1. BE PRAYED UP

One of two things will happen: either you will go to someone, or someone will come to you. So you need to be prayed up every day so that you position yourself for people to come to you. This happens a lot for me, because we travel and attend gatherings and churches where we hold altar calls for the sick. So, naturally, people come to us. Other times friends, and even strangers, are moved to ask for prayer from my wife or me. Be ready for God to move on people's hearts, and also pray for that to happen.

Being prayed up also better positions you in your relationship with the Holy Spirit. You'll know what His voice sounds like when you ask Him to heal someone or tell you what to do next. Let's be real; the more prayed up you are the more power you're going to have going into these moments. I heard a preacher once say that private prayer produces public power, and that is very true.

2. BE LOVING

If the Holy Spirit puts on your heart someone to pray for, whether that be at your grocery store or at your church, the best thing you can do for that person is show them the love of Jesus. Show love when you greet them or when asking if you can pray for them. If you don't they probably won't agree to let you pray for them, which will then nullify the whole moment. If you're reading this book you probably already love people because you want to know how to show more love through the Holy Spirit's power.

The best thing I have found when talking to strangers, or even people I know, is approaching them and telling them that I have a feeling I should pray for them. Then the ball is in their court. If they say, "No, thanks," let the Holy Spirit guide you. He may very well have you give them a word of knowledge to increase their faith, or He may just have you politely say goodbye. The only way you can know is by asking the Holy Spirit what to do. I have found that about nine out of ten times people will agree to prayer, especially if it's for something obvious like if they're walking with a limp. You will be surprised at how many people will take prayer for their hurts and sicknesses.

3. PRAY WITH EVERYTHING YOU'VE GOT

If you are prayed up this will be no problem, because you'll be operating out of the overflow of your heart and your prayer life. You don't have to be loud, crazy or pushy. In fact, that behavior usually causes people to put their guard up quite quickly. Volume doesn't affect power; faith does. I have prayed for people who have been healed within a second, and in other instances I've had to pray for someone on several different occasions before healing took place. So pray with everything you have, and if you don't know what to pray just ask the Holy Spirit, "What now?"

4. TEST IT OUT

This takes the most guts, because this is where you hand it all over to God. Remember to end the prayer when you feel like you should; there's no special length of time that it takes for someone to be healed. Kindly ask the person if they'd be willing to test out what was wrong. If they couldn't see, have them open their eyes to check if their vision has returned. If they couldn't bend a knee, have them try to do so.

As my personal rule of thumb for if they are wearing a cast or in a wheelchair, I wait for them to tell me that they want to test it out. You'll be amazed when you see their faces light up, and they'll often be surprised that the prayer actually worked.

5. GIVE JESUS THE GLORY

Once the person has tested out what was wrong and they have been healed, the best thing to do if you don't know them is to introduce them to the One who just healed them. Healing is the best way to get someone to Jesus, because it is by Jesus' love that He died for them and that same love healed them.

6. REPEAT

The math is simple. The more people you pray for, the more people who are healed. Keep praying for the sick and the sick will keep being healed. All praise and glory to Jesus!

CH 8 REFLECTION

THE BACK OF THE BOOK

Ask the Holy Spirit what He wants to do through you. I have journals that are filled with testimonies of healings, and this book can be the beginning of yours! Go out there and when these things start to happen — and they will if you're faithful — come back to this book to write down your first miracle. It won't be your last.

_____

_____

_____

_____

_____

_____

_____

_____

_____

_____

NINE: WAITING ON THE HOLY SPIRIT

Let's be honest with each other and admit that waiting is not something that anyone actually wants to do. You never hear of people looking forward to going to the DMV, or that their favorite part of Disney was the lines they got to stand in. No way. People like things now rather than later, and they want them how they ask for them. The problem, though, is that this isn't always how the Holy Spirit works. Sometimes He allows things to happen immediately and just the way we think they are going to go, but if it were always like that then we would be the god. I believe that we all say we want to become more patient people, and that we all want to learn how to wait on the Holy Spirit.

But they that wait upon the Lord shall renew their strength; they shall mount up with wings as eagles; they shall run, and not be weary; and they shall walk, and not faint.
Isaiah 40:31 KJV

Waiting on the Holy Spirit is how we learn what to do next, and not just in a moment of ministering to others. We typically hear the Holy Spirit best when we wait on Him. When we wait, we position ourselves to hear from Him and give Him the time to speak. When my prayers are full of me talking and not listening, that's a good sign that I'm not waiting on the Lord for anything. I realize that waiting is hard. Being told what to do is hard when living in a world that is all about independency and figuring things out for oneself.

Waiting can be frustrating, but it's always worth it. Think about when you go to the doctor. Do you wait? Yes, because you know that even if it takes him or her an hour to get to you, you'll get what you need. The experience isn't always what you think it's going to be, but you go because they know better. The Holy Spirit knows better than us because He knows everything; the Holy Spirit is God. The question is: why do we wait?

FIVE REASONS WHY WE HAVE TO WAIT ON GOD

1. WAITING SHOWS WHY WE WAIT

When I am waiting for something, I realize that the worth is in the wait. For example, if I went to the store to buy a candy bar — just one candy bar — but ten people were ahead of me in the line, I would probably leave because my candy bar isn't worth the wait. On the other hand, if someone were handing out ten thousand dollars to every person who wanted it and ten thousand people were ahead of me in the line, I would probably still wait for even a day or two because it would be worth the wait.

I believe that a big reason why God has us wait for things, like an answer to a big question or a spouse or kids, is because it reveals our true motives and shows if we are really willing to wait. If we are able to wait often, that says a lot to God about our trust in Him.

When I was going to college I would joke with my friends that, statistically speaking, my wife was on our campus; therefore, I should be nice to every girl. I came to find that my wife actually wasn't there, and a fun fact is that my wife graduated college when I was still in the middle of high school. My wife had graduated college and changed her career three times before we met. She'd been waiting for a long time to get married;

however, we believe that God made us for one another, so the wait was most certainly worth our while.

2. WAITNG BUILDS PATIENCE

We all know that trying to be patient in the waiting is something we hate. Have you ever been in conversation with someone who just never stops talking? You need to go somewhere, but he doesn't even seem to breathe between his sentences? I think that's one way to look at this. Having to be patient can be annoying but, like I mentioned earlier, the worth is in the wait.

The patience we have in the small things prepares us for waiting on the big things. Patience also helps us prioritize because while you wait on a response for one situation, you can work on something else for which you already have an answer.

3. WAITING BUILDS ANTICIPATION

Anticipation can be one of the greatest feelings for a person. It builds excitement and, as your anticipation grows, your expectations follow. Once you finally know that you've heard from God after waiting on Him for hours, days or even years, all the time will have been worth it. More often than not, it's also rewarding. The reward is usually in what you do, because you've waited on the Holy Spirit for His response to something and you can serve in a better capacity.

When you don't wait you end up trying to figure everything out yourself, but when you wait and do what God says to do you're golden.

4. WAITING SHAPES WHO WE ARE

I believe that who we are is determined by how we wait, and what we wait on. We rob ourselves of an opportunity to see significance in our lives the moment we stop waiting for one thing and move on to the next because it's quicker or easier. This may sound extreme, but think about the biggest decisions you make: whom you marry, buying a house, starting a family and, of course, beginning a relationship with Jesus. I would certainly hope that you don't make those decisions without taking your time beforehand. Not always but most often when things go wrong in someone's life, the events can often be sourced back to not waiting on the better option. People may marry someone very quickly and realize they married someone different than they thought, or buy the first house they see and end up having to fix it all. Some people wait until they feel the timing is convenient to have a relationship with Jesus, but they pass before they get there. Waiting can give us whole new lives. Not waiting can take our lives away from us and instead of living life, before we know it we are attempting to fix past impatient decisions over and over again.

Waiting shapes who we are, but it also shapes who we become. If you haven't been one to wait you should try it and see how it turns out. It's not too late to wait.

5. WAITING BUILDS DEPENDENCY ON GOD

Waiting is great, but waiting on God is better. I joke with my wife a lot because I am almost always early, and even when she's on time I end up waiting on her. But that's not really fair is it? No, and that's often what we tend to do with God. We try to get to where we're going faster than we need to be, and we end up waiting on God when He's still somewhere else in our lives. When we depend on ourselves instead of choosing to wait on God, all we get is a life full of ourselves.

Waiting creates intimacy and dependence on God, just like when you're a kid waiting for dad or mom to pick you up from school. If you'd had to walk instead of having them drive you, you most likely would've gotten lost and it could've taken hours longer for you to get home. Once I was waiting for my Dad to pick me up from school, and he was running a little late. I figured I could walk home; it took me forty-five minutes to walk a distance that takes five minutes to drive. I later found out that he had arrived at my school right after I'd left. I lost that forty-five minutes that could've been better spent. Waiting on God is like waiting to be picked up in a car or bus. We wait because we know that once the bus arrives we'll go faster than we ever could on foot.

HOW TO WAIT ON THE HOLY SPIRIT

The Bible is the best place for everything, and we shouldn't be surprised that in it we will find our answer of how to best wait on the Holy Spirit. When I think of stories that involve waiting on God in the Bible (and most stories involve this), the first one I think of is the story of Moses — not because of how long he waited, but how many times he waited. Moses demanded of Pharaoh to let his people go, yet Pharaoh declined time after time and eight more times. Moses had to ask ten times for something that was very much of God. His story reveals that just because people aren't on board with God's plan doesn't mean that the plan isn't God's.

Here's what is crazy to me about Moses: not only did he wait ten times for the same thing, but he had to watch people — people he would've known from his past life — be tormented and killed through the ten plagues. There is a way to wait on God and it may seem simple, but waiting comes down to faith. The greater your faith the shorter the wait will feel. If you know that God is Lord and will come through on His promises, then waiting will become less of an issue in your life and will actually become a benefit. A relationship with the Holy Spirit is built on faith and lasts on obedience.

A different way of looking at waiting is referring to it as obedience. When waiting seems too difficult of a task for me, I end up telling myself that I am not simply waiting but obeying. The idea of waiting in any situation often has a lot of frustrating connotations; however, hearing something from God should excite us. We should not hesitate to respond and do what the Lord has told us to do. The next time that God tells you to wait, remind yourself that waiting is obeying and there is a reason for the wait.

CH 9 REFLECTION

WAIT A MINUTE

Start asking God what it looks like for you to wait on Him and, better yet, ask Him how to fulfill your emotional needs during this time. Waiting can be difficult so rely on the Holy Spirit to guide your thoughts, and have your faith pointed toward the end goal even if you don't yet know what it is.

_____

_____

_____

_____

_____

_____

_____

_____

_____

TEN: LEARNING TO FAIL

Waiting can be difficult, but the effects of failing are far more painful and lasting. That doesn't have to be the case when dealing with the Holy Spirit. Remember, He's not a bird. He's on your team and you're on His. He won't let you down. Failing is something that all people dread; you may have never felt good while failing, but that's all about to change.

THREE REASONS WHY FAILING IS HEALTHY

1. FAILING GIVES PERSPECTIVE

Failure can be one of the most beneficial attributes of someone who spreads the Gospel, because it makes us smaller and makes God that much bigger. That failing, especially on a spiritual level, would make God bigger may seem bizarre, but just think of how many times we all failed at learning to walk as babies. The only way we figured it out was through failing, and now we walk without even having to think about it.

The fear of failure in regard to spiritual gifts, such as praying for the sick and seeing them not get healed, is quite silly because God doesn't fail. He plans. God's thoughts are higher than mine, so when someone doesn't get healed I don't ask God why they weren't healed. I ask how I can grow in faith, and I ask Him to give me understanding or insight as to why. He doesn't always tell me exactly, but He will often give me a glimpse at why He will later.

Failing shows me that healing doesn't come from me. The power to heal the sick is not my power; otherwise, I would be a god. I am drawn closer to God whenever I pray for the sick and they aren't healed.

2. FAILING KILLS FEAR

Fear is one of humanity's strongest feelings. Fear can stop everything that we do, and it can save our lives. If you were to suddenly see a car about to hit you, your first response would be fear. Fear is what triggers our bodies to move out of the way in order to save us. Fear can be good, but it is often evil; fear is belief in a lie that you are afraid will come true.

Once I had failed enough times, I was no longer afraid of it. In fact, I now welcome it. I realized that I blamed myself the first couple times that I prayed for sick people and they didn't get healed. I'd become upset that my power wasn't great enough. As you probably already know, this isn't healthy. Failing caused me to see that I was portraying myself as powerful because of my pride. I now look at failure as an opportunity to see that I'm not working in my own power, but that I am simply a vessel for God's power to work through.

Being afraid of failing in regard to the gifts of the Spirit is actually a much deeper fear — the fear that God will let you down. Gathering your boldness and walking over to the person who God told you to speak to only to have them decline prayer can be hurtful. If you don't put your mind in alignment with the Gospel, then you'll end up being upset with God. However, if you are aligned with the Word you will understand that there are many reasons why someone may decline. Their choice doesn't mean that you were wrong; they just weren't ready for what God was about to do. Honestly, God could also be preparing you. He might just be entrusting you now to find if He will be able to trust you with much greater tasks later.

Hopefully by now you understand that failing isn't really failing. It is an opportunity to grow and learn to see we must become small so that He may become big.

3. FAILING BUILDS DEPENDENCY ON GOD

I had to fail a lot of times to realize that I was trying to do things in my own strength. Remember, failing isn't always failing. The best thing to do when you feel like you have failed, or as if you are a failure, is to ask God to speak to that feeling and what the truth is. You are not a failure and you have not failed. You just happen to be a human that cannot see outside of space and time; you are not God.

The more that you let the Holy Spirit into your life, the more you will realize how failure is a key to learning and growth. I didn't just one day start to pray for the sick and have great faith that everyone I prayed for would be healed. No, I had to fail countless times. I had to hear God telling me that I was on the right track — that the result would be worth what I'd experienced. I had to entrust myself to Him.

ENTRUST THE HOLY SPIRIT

While serving at a youth service where I was asked to pray for the sick, I got on stage and God's presence was clearly there — no doubt about it. Students were going after Jesus on a whole new level. I got on the microphone and began to pray that the

Holy Spirit would empower the students to perform miracles, and that they would see their friends, family and others in that auditorium instantly healed. Soon after that I told the students that I believed that God wanted to heal people with back problems. A little over ten students came to the front of the altar and all were miraculously healed. One of the college students who was a youth leader had a back problem that had lasted years. She couldn't even remember the last time she wasn't in pain. She was healed so quickly and powerfully that we asked her to give her testimony to the hundreds of other students who were watching.

She started telling a story of how long she'd been in pain, and how difficult it was to even sleep at night. I'd asked how she was feeling on a pain scale of one to ten before I'd prayed for her, and she told everyone that it was about a five. At that point, the pain was halfway to being the worst of her life and she'd dealt with it for years. I then asked how she was feeling on that pain scale after we prayed. With tears in her eyes she was able to tell hundreds of students that Jesus healed her back!

The night had already been full of awesome healings, but the Holy Spirit wasn't yet done. Earlier in the service my wife, who was sitting next to me, told me that she was feeling that God was going to heal ears. I told her I felt the same, but as I was on the stage I didn't know if that was the night He wanted to do so. When I was praying again the Holy Spirit suddenly prompted me to pray for someone with a deaf ear. I got on the microphone and told the students that I believed that someone in the room was deaf in one ear, and that he needed to raise his hand so I could come pray for him. No hands rose. God then began to show me where the young man was in the room. So I told everyone that I believed it was a boy, and still no hands went up. Then I told the students that I believed he was standing on the right side of the auditorium. Again, no hands rose. Finally, God told me exactly where he was. Once more I implored the students that there was a boy in the back of the auditorium on the far right side who needed to be healed of deafness in one ear. No hands rose. Honestly, I felt pretty silly; I felt as though I'd failed.

The service came to a close and I was getting ready to apologize to my friend who was the youth pastor. As I started walking on the stage, a young man approached me and hugged me. I had no idea what was going on initially, but as I turned around I realized that he was crying and that something was going on. I brought my wife over so that we could minister together, and this senior in high school said, "I'm the guy." He then told me that he was embarrassed to come to the front, and that he'd had back pain for years. Catch this. He was also deaf in one ear. God had told me that there were people in the room with back pain, and that there were some with deaf ears. The young man I was talking to had all of the symptoms that God wanted to heal that night. Where had he been standing? He was in the back on the right side of the room. Surprise! God was right.

What I have learned is that failure isn't something to fear, because we never know if we have actually failed. The truth is that if we are obedient to God, failure is nearly impossible. The student's back and ear were both miraculously healed. He was able to hear in both of his ears for the first time since he was a child.

Don't just trust the Holy Spirit; entrust the Holy Spirit. Believing in Him means trusting who He is. Letting Him in means entrusting that He is who He says He is. Trust is what you take, while entrusting is what you give. Once you move from taking to giving, the Holy Spirit moves from being some bird that's in a cage to the God who can fully love you and take you to higher places than any bird ever could.

YOUR ADVENTURE

This is where you can write down anything that the Holy Spirit has done through you since you started reading this book. My prayer is that you fill it with testimonies of miracles that happen because of your faith. Go get 'em!

_____

_____

_____

_____

_____

_____

_____

_____

ABOUT THE AUTHOR

Ty Buckingham and his wife, Rebecca, minister on the Holy Spirit through preaching and personal altar ministry. They have seen many people filled with the Spirit, and many more miraculously healed in services and in public places.

When they preach about the Holy Spirit at churches and gatherings, people are able to experience the Holy Spirit in a simple and straightforward manner. As a result, people may easily receive both the baptism and healing without any of the weird baggage.

www.TyBuckingham.com